A GRAPHIC HISTORY OF THE CIVIL RIGHTS MOVEMENT

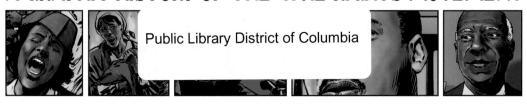

MARTIN LUTHER KING JR.
AND THE MARCH ON WASHINGTON

BY GARY JEFFREY
ILLUSTRATED BY NICK SPENDER

Gareth Stevens
Publishing

Please visit our website, www.garethstevens.com.
For a free color catalog of all our high-quality books,
call toll free 1-800-542-2595 or fax 1-877-542-2596.

Library of Congress Cataloging-in-Publication Data

Jeffrey, Gary.
Martin Luther King Jr. and the March on Washington / Gary Jeffrey.
p. cm. — (A graphic history of the civil rights movement)
Includes index.
ISBN 978-1-4339-7492-2 (pbk.)
ISBN 978-1-4339-7493-9 (6-pack)
ISBN 978-1-4339-7491-5 (library binding)
1. King, Martin Luther, Jr., 1929-1968. I have a dream—Juvenile literature.
2. March on Washington for Jobs and Freedom, Washington, D.C., 1963—
Juvenile literature. 3. Civil rights demonstrations—Washington (D.C.)—
History—20th century—Juvenile literature. 4. African Americans—Civil
rights—History—20th century—Juvenile literature. I. Title.
E185.97.K5J434 2013
323.1196'073—dc23
2011050608

First Edition

Published in 2013 by
Gareth Stevens Publishing
111 East 14th Street, Suite 349
New York, NY 10003

Designed by David West Books

Printed in the United States

CPSIA compliance information: Batch #DWS12GS: For further information contact Gareth Stevens, New York, New York at 1-800-542-2595.

CONTENTS

LET FREEDOM RING

During the 1950s, racial segregation in public schools had been successfully challenged through the courts. However, southern states were slow to integrate, and there was still no law stopping private businesses from being as racist as they liked.

President Kennedy addresses the nation on civil rights.

A SUMMER OF (NONVIOLENT) PROTEST

In May 1963, the Southern Christian Leadership Congress, led by Martin Luther King Jr., used nonviolent protest to force businesses in Birmingham, Alabama, to desegregate. The media storm surrounding the brutality of the Birmingham police tactics against the protesters also caused President Kennedy to announce a new civil rights bill.

A MARCH FOR JOBS AND FREEDOM

The SCLC and other civil rights groups wanted to keep up the pressure for change. It was decided to organize a march on the capital to demand the civil rights bill be strengthened and passed by Congress.

The marchers would also demand a complete end to segregation in schools, passage of a bill for fair employment, and a minimum wage.

In 1942, labor leader A. Philip Randolph had the idea of marching on Washington to protest armed forces' segregation, but it didn't happen.

THE VOICE OF MORAL COURAGE

Martin Luther King Jr. was born the son of a preacher in Atlanta, Georgia, in 1929. At college, King learned about the Indian leader Gandhi, who had used nonviolent protest successfully against the British. In 1954, he became the minister of Dexter Avenue Baptist Church in Montgomery, Alabama.

When Rosa Parks famously refused to give up her place on a segregated bus and was arrested in 1955, King spearheaded the resulting Montgomery boycott campaign and became one of the foremost civil rights leaders.

A powerful speaker, Martin Luther King Jr. had the ability to inspire ordinary citizens to join together and stand up for their rights.

GETTING IT TOGETHER

The biggest question was— "Would enough people come?" Organizers toiled to publicize the march and arrange transportation. Most would come from the North, with a few brave souls from the South. Along with the other leaders, Martin Luther King Jr. worked up a speech with which to address the crowd...

Civil rights organizers set up headquarters in Washington, D.C.

NATIONAL HEADQUARTERS

MARCH
ON
WASHINGTON
FOR **JOBS**
& **FREEDOM**

WED. AUG. 28

MARTIN LUTHER KING JR. AND THE MARCH ON WASHINGTON

AUGUST 28, 1963, WASHINGTON, D.C.

FROM ALL OVER AMERICA THEY HAD COME. MORE THAN 250,000, MOSTLY AFRICAN AMERICAN, WITH A FEW THOUSAND WHITE SUPPORTERS JOINING THEM.

GLORY, GLORY, HALLELUJAH! GLORY, GLORY, HALLELUJAH! HIS TRUTH IS MARCHING ON.

FORWARD THEY MARCHED. FROM THE WASHINGTON MONUMENT TOWARD THE LINCOLN MEMORIAL, UNITED BY THE "BATTLE HYMN OF THE REPUBLIC."

HE IS COMING LIKE THE GLORY OF THE MORNING ON THE WAVE, HE IS WISDOM TO THE MIGHTY, HE IS SUCCOR TO THE BRAVE...

SCORES OF TELEVISION CAMERAS CAPTURED THE SCENE.

...HIS DAY IS MARCHING ON.

KING WENT ON TO DECLARE THAT 100 YEARS LATER, AFRICAN AMERICANS WERE STILL NOT FREE, AND TALKED ABOUT HOW, WITH THE DECLARATION OF INDEPENDENCE, THE FOUNDING FATHERS HAD GIVEN A **PROMISE** THAT...

...**ALL** MEN, YES, **BLACK** MEN AS WELL AS **WHITE** MEN, WOULD BE GUARANTEED THE **UNALIENABLE RIGHTS** OF LIFE, LIBERTY, AND THE PURSUIT OF HAPPINESS.

HE SAID THAT AMERICA, INSTEAD OF **HONORING** THIS PROMISE...

...HAS GIVEN THE NEGRO PEOPLE A **BAD CHECK**...

...A CHECK WHICH HAS COME BACK MARKED *"INSUFFICIENT FUNDS."*

WHILE KING REMINDED THE CROWD OF THE **URGENCY** OF THE CIVIL RIGHTS MISSION, HE ALSO COUNSELLED THEM TO BE **PEACEFUL**...

LET US NOT SATISFY OUR THIRST FOR FREEDOM BY DRINKING FROM THE CUP OF **BITTERNESS** AND **HATRED.**

HE REMINDED THE PROTESTERS NOT TO DISTRUST ALL WHITE PEOPLE, THAT THE TWO RACES' DESTINIES WERE **TIED TOGETHER.**

THERE ARE THOSE WHO ARE ASKING US, *"WHEN WILL YOU BE SATISFIED?"*

KING WENT ON TO LIST THEIR DISSATISFACTIONS, TALKING OF POLICE BRUTALITY AND THE HUMILIATION OF JIM CROW, AND ENDING WITH THE ISSUE OF *THE VOTE*...

WE CANNOT BE SATISFIED AS LONG AS A NEGRO IN MISSISSIPPI *CANNOT* VOTE AND A NEGRO IN NEW YORK BELIEVES HE HAS NOTHING FOR WHICH TO VOTE.

ALRIGHT!

TELL IT, DOCTOR!

KING LEVELLED HIS GAZE AT THE CROWD AND PREPARED TO SPEAK *FROM THE HEART.*

HIS VOICE RISING, KING MADE A PLEA TO LET FREEDOM **RING OUT**...

...FROM THE MANY HILLTOPS OF NEW HAMPSHIRE...

...THE MIGHTY MOUNTAINS OF NEW YORK...

...STONE MOUNTAIN OF GEORGIA...

...LOOKOUT MOUNTAIN OF TENNESSEE...

...AND EVERY HILL AND MOLEHILL OF MISSISSIPPI...

WHEN WE ALLOW FREEDOM TO **RING**, WE WILL SPEED UP THAT DAY WHEN **ALL** WILL BE ABLE TO JOIN HANDS AND **SING**...

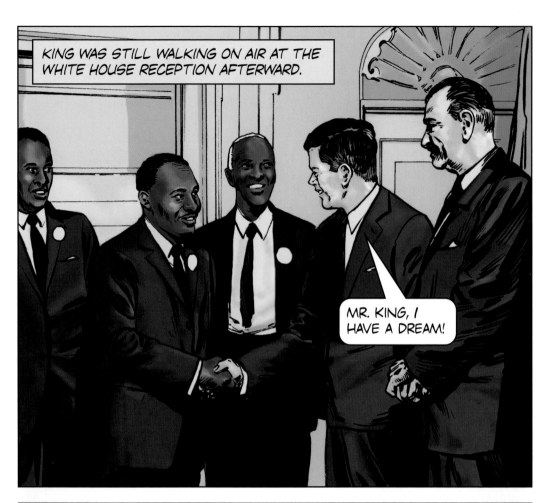

KING WAS STILL WALKING ON AIR AT THE WHITE HOUSE RECEPTION AFTERWARD.

MR. KING, I HAVE A DREAM!

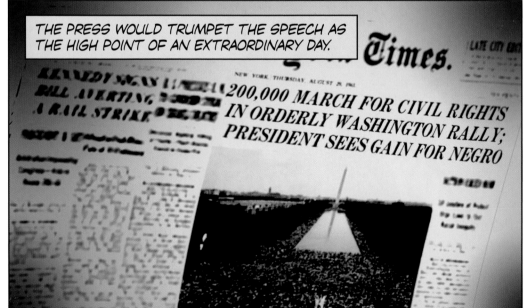

THE PRESS WOULD TRUMPET THE SPEECH AS THE HIGH POINT OF AN EXTRAORDINARY DAY.

MEANWHILE, THAT EVENING KING SOUGHT OUT A. PHILIP RANDOLPH TO CONGRATULATE HIM.

WELL, MR RANDOLPH, YOU FINALLY *GOT* YOUR MARCH...

...AFTER ALL THESE YEARS.

THE MARCH OF FATE

The march was covered by more than 500 television cameras. King's electrifying speech was heard across the nation and did much to stir the consciences of decent white Americans both north and south.

ENDINGS AND BEGINNINGS

As his civil rights bill struggled through Congress, Kennedy was suddenly shot dead while visiting Dallas, Texas, on November 22, 1963. Vice President Lyndon B. Johnson was sworn in and vowed to get the civil rights legislation through "as a memorial to the late President."

King watches President Johnson sign the 1964 civil rights act into law. After campaigns in the Deep South, the voting rights act would follow in 1965.

MAN OF THE YEAR

King himself was made Time Magazine's Man of the Year in 1963 and awarded the Nobel Peace Prize in 1964. King continued to be a major force in the civil rights movement and was planning a mass demonstration in Washington to highlight African American poverty when he was cruelly cut down by a sniper's bullet in Memphis, Tennessee, on April 4, 1968. More than 60,000 people attended his funeral in Atlanta.

King continues to be an inspirational figure for civil rights campaigners the world over. His Washington speech is regarded as one of the greatest speeches of all time.

GLOSSARY

boycott To refuse to buy a product or use a service because of political reasons.

brutality Violence.

conscience A person's sense of right and wrong.

creed A set of beliefs, usually written down and recited.

emancipator One who sets people free.

rostrum A platform or podium from which speeches are delivered.

score Twenty.

segregation The forced separation of blacks and whites in public.

spearheaded Led, took charge of.

succor Support during a difficult time.

unalienable Not able to be taken away.

urgency The need to act quickly.

INDEX